I0099283

Seriously Serial

Also by John J. Trause

Eye Candy for Andy
Georgetown, KY: Finishing Line Press, 2013

Inside Out, Upside Down & Round and Round
Daryaganj, New Delhi: Nirala Publications, 2012

Latter-Day Litany
Maywood, NJ: Éditions élastiques, 1996

Seriously Serial

Poems by

John J. Trause

POETS WEAR PRADA • Hoboken, New Jersey

Seriously Serial

Copyright © 2007 John J. Trause

All rights reserved. Except for use in any review or for educational purposes, the reproduction or utilization of this work in whole or in part in any form by electronic, mechanical or other means, now known or hereafter invented, including xerography, photocopying and recording, or in any informational or retrieval system, is forbidden without the written permission of the publisher:

Poets Wear Prada
533 Bloomfield Street, Second Floor
Hoboken, New Jersey 07030
http://pwpbooks.blogspot.com

First North American Publication 2007
First Mass Market Paperback Edition 2013

Grateful acknowledgment is made to *Global City Review* and *Sidereality: A Journal of Speculative and Experimental Poetry* where some of these poems have previously appeared. And to Jill Greenberg for permission to reproduce selected images from her ongoing *Accumulation Project* (2005 –).

ISBN-13: 978-0615863580
ISBN-10: 0615863582

Printed in the U.S.A.

Front Cover: Digitally altered detail of "The Sweetest Fruit," soap sliver mosaic, Jill Greenberg, 2006

Back Cover Author Photo: Jill Greenberg, 2007

This Little Book Is Dedicated To:

છ

John XXIII (Angelo Roncalli), Pope 1958 – 1963;
Irreverent literary gamesters;
Lesbians of the world and Lewis Carroll;
Leonardo da Vinci; Lucille Ball, who died on my birthday;
*   and Carol Burnett, who shares my birthday;*
Gertrude Stein;
Rafinesque;
Eratosthenes of Cyrene and Callimachus of Cyrene;
Eliot, T. S.; and Elliot, Mama Cass;
Nabokov, Vladimir; and Vivian Darkbloom;
Bernd and Hilla Becher;
Endless variations and various exoticisms;
Rod Serling;
God.

છ

Per saecula saeculorum

છ

Table of Contents

Illustrations

NOTE: All the images are from Jill Greenberg's ongoing *Accumulation Project* (2005 –).

Seriously Serial

Laudato sie, mi' Signore, cum tucte le tue creature

— St. Francis of Assisi

Indeed, both in society at large and in the categories of signs we can see at work a basic human impulse that can be called "the taxonomic urge."

— Tom McArthur, *Worlds of Reference* (1986)

Compass Point Poems

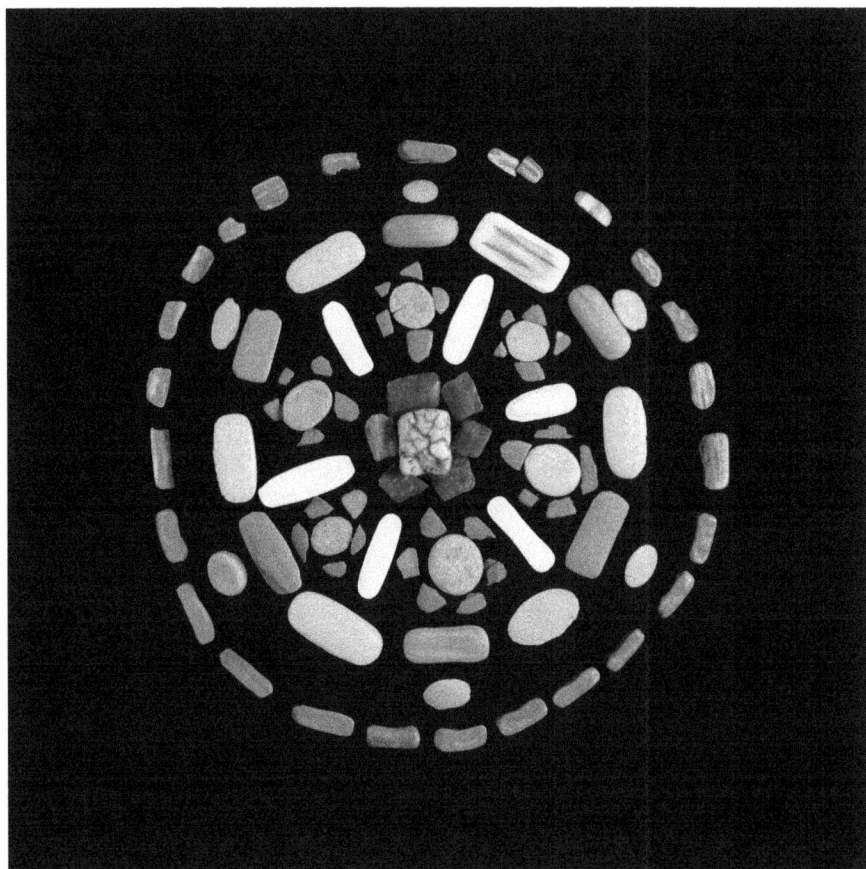

In the American West

In the American West
three sheep
hang in a
slaughterhouse,
their heads
hanging
like purple
wisteria

NOTE: Inspired by Richard Avedon's photograph of three sheep in a
slaughterhouse in Ennis, Montana, published in *In the American West*
(1985).

In the North of Europe

Norway
Sweden
Finland
hang in the sea,
their masses
hanging
like
auto-
erotic
suicides

In East Berlin

In East Berlin
a wall stands
a wall stands
still a wall stands,
the hands that
made it tearing
it down

In the South of Gotham

In the
south
of
Gotham   In the
two   south
towers   of the   smoke
stand   city
tall,   two
their   towers
masses   smoke
narrow,   like
glinting   stubbed
like a   butts
remote   in an
control   ashtray   ash   ashes

East or West

Whether I'm on the
East or West side
of the City, and
depending on the time and day,
the weather,
and the slant of the sun in the sky,
I either bless or curse
Robert Moses for laying down the law
and this highway.

Daughters of the Revolution

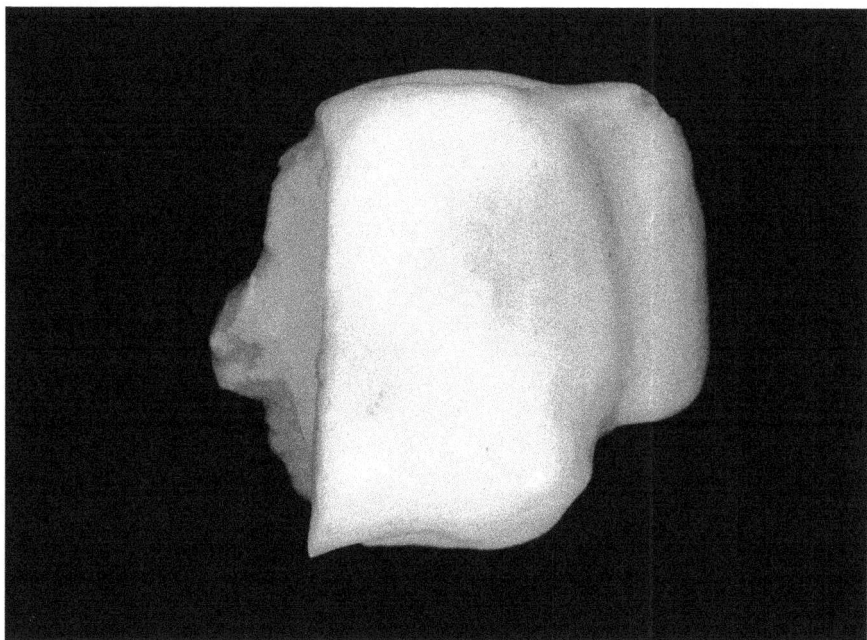

Patricia Hearst

"growing"

Planted in the ground of a locked closet
she grows in the dark,
growing up to be
a movie star.

Abigail Folger

"flowing"

Raw war runs red, raging over a white dress
against the sodden lawn of Sodom,
her blood flowing, ceases
like a slaked riverbed in arid L.A.,
a glutted heiress of affluence who inherits
not a fortune in coffee, but
a throatful of gore and a red dress.

Linda Rae Fitzpatrick

"blowing"

The night has powers of transformation
as a cool night in October
transforms a Connecticut heiress
into not just a statistic, but
a symbol of youth blown out
on the boiler-room floor of a flyblown
tenement flat on Avenue B,
blowing Groovy, her head blown out
by speed and speedy violence,
seedy as the mattress she died on.

Gamble Benedict

"stowing"

Little girl lost at sea, a castaway
turned stowaway,
can be found hitched up somewhere
and stowing away in her honeymoon hideout
in the Marlboro Inn in Montclair
just around the corner from here,
an heiress who burns away her stash
in an inflammatory conubium.

Edith Sedgwick

"snowing" / "showing" / "glowing"

Where is she?   Tucked away at Silver Hill,
her connection in Connecticut (snowing),
or showing on the silver screen,
glowing silver in the Factory,
silver-haired like Andy, eye candy for all,
the quintessence of the hipness of cool
or the coolness of hip.
This youthquaker rises to the screen
ethereal, reflected spectacularly
in the silver tinsel, and behind the tinsel —
barbed wire.

More Daughters of the Revolution

Footnotes for the Chinese

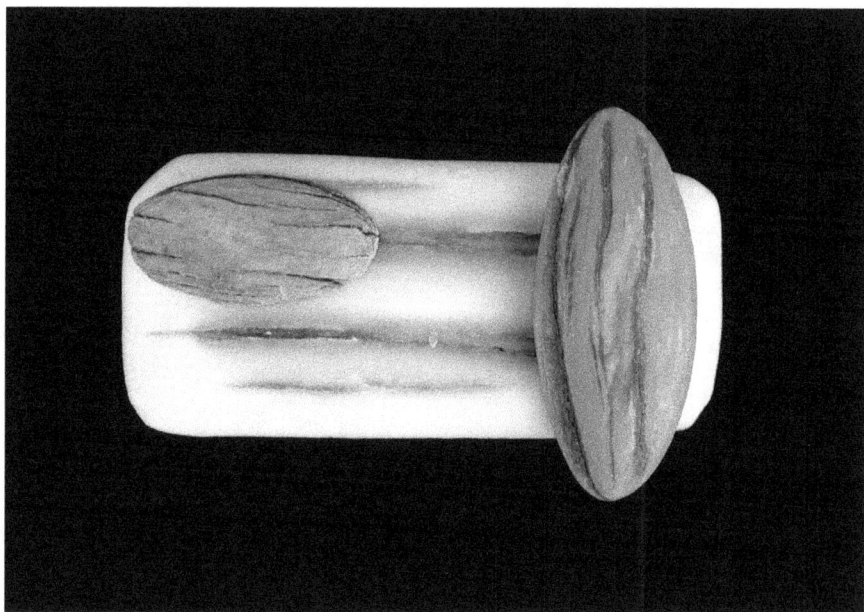

Doris Duke / Barbara Hutton

"knowing"

She knows what many others know
of the dark wood,
the golden flower,
and the land
where Porfirio
Rubirosa grows wild,
exotic and always
ready. She is ready
to give it away,
and she would,
a dime at a time.

Elizabeth Grubman

"mowing"

In the Hamptons,
outside the Inn of Conscience,
without conscience or consciousness,
with the pedal to the metal,
mowing the crowd down,
she shows who's boss.
It's a toss up.

Ways of Unbeing

Ethereal Sharon

Flesh drained of its bloated bulge
and bulldozing bombast
remains in suspended animation on its hospital bed,
dozing.
Oh you who strutted proud on the Temple Mount
are now a mound of tempered pride,
your spirit drifting, drifting up,
up over the Golan Heights,
a massive embolism in the sky
aerial and ethereal.
no more threats; condition stable.

Go on the Lam, Cipel

Alexander had his Bagōas;
Hadrian his Antinoüs;
McGreevey had his Golan
until all hell broke loose.
You could have been drowned in the Delaware,
a boating party, and become a god.
Go on the lam, Cipel,
back to the security of your homeland,
where you know that silence equals death.

Anthony
Joel
Lee

He manifested himself amid the
manifestos of the Nuyorican,
slender and tender, a reed bent
but not broken at the confluence
of the Red and Assiniboine,
muddy waters of Winnipeg,
weathered by life along the Hudson.
By the waters of the Passaic dashing
on the rocks below, you rock.
By the lazy currents of Tan-shui and
Chi-lung, you rock.
By the Narrows of Saint John's, you rock
and flow and go with the flow,
cyber-singing on the ethernet,
here now, now gone,
there in that bit of cybertext
silent, there in the flickering
still, evanescing here now,
in the stillness, ethereal there
tuning to the music of the spheres.

Dakotastasis

The lights, the lights too bright
the night she sang at Memories,
too bright, and so she stood and stared
and reappeared and sang round midnight.
The lights too bright after years of memories,
the late late show, the lurid glow,
and lithium and life amid that dimly lit,
starlit, barlit, twilight time, staring
at the frozen faces of friends and fans,
so far between then and now in twilight time,
suspended in a state of stasis.
Dakota Staton, stay.

The Poet Himself
November 1993

Imagining himself on the second night of
three consecutive nights of fever dreams
to be transformed bodily into an English countryside,
divided, squared, hedgerowed,
ploughed this way and that,
some parts fertile, some fallow,
he seems by seams to be disassembled at the
    forehead
    upper lip
    neck
    diaphragm
    waist
    hips
    knees
    ankles
    toes
and in between, crisscrossed,
patched and quilted, furrowed
forward and back, punctuated by stiles
over the dividing walls and hedges.
The worry is, the grinding worry and anxiety,
is that one may not be reassembled properly
in the course of this transformational nightmare.
Old dream maker, you part breaker,
you're crossing me by stile one night.

Acknowledgments

I wish to thank the members of The Writers Group and of The Poetry Group who have read and provided suggestions on the poems included herein.

I wish to thank for their impeccable taste and vision the publishers and editors of the journals who have already published or will be publishing some of these poems included herein. "In the American West" first appeared in *Global City Review*. The poems contained in "Daughters of the Revolution" and "More Daughters of the Revolution" were previously published by *Sidereality: A Journal of Speculative and Experimental Poetry*.

I wish to thank especially Roxanne Hoffman of Poets Wear Prada for her encouragement, patience, hard work, professionalism, perfectionism, and fun along the way in bringing this project to the sweetest fruition.

I wish to thank Jill Greenberg for helping to make a very interesting project even more complex and for making a very complex life even more interesting.

About the Author

JOHN J. TRAUSE, Director of Oradell Public Library in Oradell, New Jersey, since 2010 and formerly Director of the Wood-Ridge Memorial Library in Wood-Ridge, New Jersey, from 2000 to 2010, has been writing and reciting his poetry for over thirty years. The Serials Librarian (seriously) at the Museum of Modern Art Library from 1991 to 2000, and a participant in The MoMA Strike of 2000, he has been an active part of the New York art scene as well as an avid devotee of avant-garde public raucousness.

His poetry, translations, and visual work have appeared in *Cover*, *Global City Review*, *Parse*, *Radix*, *The Rift*, *Now Culture*, *Sensations Magazine*, *The North River Review*, *The Troubadour*, *Xavier Review*, the artists' periodical *Crossings* published by the Brooklyn Waterfront Artists Coalition, as well as online in *The Pedestal Magazine* and *Sidereality*, and many other print and online journals and anthologies, published nationally and internationally. His monumental performance poem *Ishtar Redux* was staged in 2001 at the renovated Journal Square Loews Theatre in Jersey City, New Jersey, and in 2013 at La MaMa Experimental Theatre Club in New York. His *Latter-Day Litany and Other Pseudo-Hagiographica* has had a number of revivals after its New York debut in 1998, most recently in 2004 at the Bickford Theatre at the Morris Museum, Morristown, New Jersey. In 2005 and again in 2006, Mr. Trause was featured at Stevens Institute of Technology in Hoboken, New Jersey, in the *Visible Word* exhibition which paired poets with visual artists. In 2005 he co-founded the William Carlos Williams Poetry Cooperative in Rutherford, New Jersey, where he served as programmer and host until 2012.

Aside from his professional interest in literature and the arts, Mr. Trause also enjoys film, dance, juggling, hiking, Chinese footbinding, and Afrin® nasal spray. In his adolescence, he modeled for the monolithic sculptures on Easter Island.

About the Artist

Born in Baton Rouge, Louisiana, **JILL GREENBERG** retains no vestige of her southern heritage other than her ability to endure extreme "humiture" with minimal perspiration, and her distinct preference for the fluid plural pronoun "y'all" over the nasal Northeastern version, "you guys!" Her family moved to Cincinnati, Ohio, where she attended one of the few remaining public high schools requiring the study of Latin, which later became one of the many threads of fate connecting her to poet John J. Trause.

Jill attended University of Virginia her freshman year, where she studied literature and art history. She left U.Va. to study fine art photography, film, and sculpture at the University of Cincinnati, where she met poet John J. Trause.

She worked as a photographer for the *The Philadelphia Inquirer* during the decade that spanned the industry's transition from film to digital technology. Ms. Greenberg left her position there in 2001 to earn her Master of Fine Arts degree in mixed media art at Baltimore's renowned Maryland Institute College of Art.

Known for her inventive use of non-traditional art materials, such as soap slivers, dandelion fluff, molted cicada "shells," and plastic packaging, she has received Individual Artist grants from the Maryland State Arts Council, the City of Baltimore Arts and Humanities, and in 2008 was awarded an Alumni Travel Grant to visit various locations in England and Spain by the Center for Emerging Visual Artists in Philadelphia. Ms. Greenberg's art has been exhibited extensively along the East Coast, as well as the Midwest and South, and she has worked as a tutor and teacher of writing, photography, and art.

About the Accumulation Project

In September 2005, the Brooklyn artists' collective *Other Leading Brand* challenged 20 artists each to accumulate an object for a year, and to make art with the resulting collection. Jill Greenberg chose to accumulate the used remains of bar soap, commonly known as "soap slivers," and found the work so rewarding that she is continuing her project indefinitely. To contribute your soap slivers, please contact Jill Greenberg at jillgreenberg27@hotmail.com. Visit the official *Accumulation Project* website at www.accumulationproject.org.

A Note on the Type

This book was set in Garamond Macron, designed by Paul Kennett and available from the Māori Law Review site. A macron, from the Greek μακρόν (*makrón*), meaning "long," is a short, straight, horizontal mark [-] placed above a vowel to indicate a long sound or over a syllable to indicate a stressed or long syllable in a metrical foot.

www.ingramcontent.com/pod-product-compliance
Lightning Source LLC
Chambersburg PA
CBHW061758040426
42447CB00011B/2370

* 9 7 8 0 6 1 5 8 6 3 5 8 0 *